D0498318

JUNGLE BABIES
of the Amazon
Rain Forest

Three-Toed Sloths

by Rachel Lynette

Consultant:
Dr. Mark C. Andersen
Department of Fish, Wildlife and Conservation Ecology
New Mexico State University

BEARPORT
PUBLISHING

New York, New York

Credits

Cover and Title, © Matthew W. Keefe/Shutterstock Images; 4–5, © age fotostock/
SuperStock; 6, © Red Line Editorial; 6–7, © Minden Pictures/SuperStock; 8, © Red Line
Editorial; 8–9, © NHPA/SuperStock; 10–11, © Minden Pictures/SuperStock; 12–13, ©
Thomas Haupt/imagebro/imagebroker.net/SuperStock; 14–15, © Minden Pictures/
SuperStock; 16–17, © Jouan & Rius/naturepl.com; 18, 23 (top), © worldswildlifewonders/
Shutterstock Images; 18–19, 22 (top), © BMJ/Shutterstock Images; 20–21, © Piper
Mackay/naturepl.com; 22 (bottom), © NHPA/SuperStock; 23 (bottom), © AND Inc./
Shutterstock Images.

Publisher: Kenn Goin
Editor: Joy Bean
Creative Director: Spencer Brinker
Photo Researcher: Arnold Ringstad
Design: Emily Love

Library of Congress Cataloging-in-Publication Data

Lynette, Rachel.
  Three-toed sloths / by Rachel Lynette.
    pages cm. — (Jungle babies of the Amazon rain forest)
  Includes bibliographical references and index.
  Audience: Ages 6-9.
  ISBN-13: 978-1-61772-756-6 (library binding)
  ISBN-10: 1-61772-756-3 (library binding)
  1. Bradypus tridactylus—Juvenile literature. I. Title.
  QL737.E22L96 2013
  599.3'13—dc23
                        2012039867

For more information, write to Bearport Publishing Company, Inc., 45 West 21st Street,
Suite 3B, New York, New York 10010. Printed in the United States of America.

10 9 8 7 6 5 4 3 2 1

Contents

Meet a three-toed sloth

After spending hours looking for fruit to eat, a mother three-toed sloth is tired.

To rest, she hangs from a high tree branch with her baby clinging to her belly.

Soon, she and the baby will fall asleep.

mother

baby

What is a three-toed sloth?

A three-toed sloth is a small **mammal**.

It has thick brown fur.

Adult three-toed sloth size

It also has three claws on each front foot.

An adult weighs about ten pounds (4.5 kg).

A baby weighs just a half pound (0.2 kg).

claws

Where do three-toed sloths live?

Three-toed sloths can be found in Central and South America.

They live in the treetops of **rain forests**.

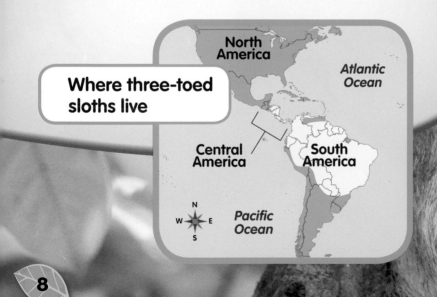

Where three-toed sloths live

North America

Atlantic Ocean

Central America

South America

N W E S

Pacific Ocean

8

A baby three-toed sloth spends its days with its mother among the tree branches.

9

At home in the trees

Three-toed sloths have long, curved claws.

They use their claws to climb.

They also use them to hold on to tree branches as they hang upside down.

Three-toed sloths only come down to the ground to go to the bathroom.

They do this about once a week.

sloth hanging
from a tree branch

Slow and sleepy

Three-toed sloths are the slowest mammals on Earth.

They do not move very often and never run or jump.

Baby three-toed sloths move even slower than adults.

Both adults and babies spend most of their time sleeping.

They sometimes sleep for up to twenty hours a day!

A new baby

A mother three-toed sloth gives birth while hanging upside down.

She has just one baby at a time.

The baby clings to its mother's belly as soon as it is born.

It stays there for its first nine months of life.

For about six weeks, the mother feeds the baby milk from her body.

baby clinging to mother's belly

15

Time to eat

Three-toed sloths eat mostly leaves and fruits.

A baby three-toed sloth learns what to eat by watching its mother.

When it is a few months old, the baby starts to reach for nearby food.

As it grows bigger, it leaves its mother to search for food on its own.

Blending in

Even though sloths have brown fur, they often look a little green.

That is because **algae** grow on the sloths' fur.

The green algae help the sloths blend in with the green trees.

Predators such as harpy eagles find it hard to spot the green animals.

harpy eagle

Algae start to grow on a baby's fur when the baby is a few weeks old.

All grown up

A three-toed sloth stays with its mother for about two years.

Once the baby is grown, the mother moves to a different part of the jungle.

The newly grown-up sloth, however, stays in its mother's old area.

By age three, a female sloth can have a baby.

When the new baby arrives, it too will learn all about life in the treetops.

adult sloth

Glossary

algae (AL-jee)
tiny plant-like living things that grow in water or on damp surfaces

mammal (MAM-uhl)
a warm-blooded animal that has hair and drinks its mother's milk as a baby

predators
(PRED-uh-turz)
animals that hunt
and eat other
animals

rain forests
(RAYN FOR-ists)
large, warm areas
of land covered with
trees and plants,
where lots of rain falls

Index

Read more

Clark, Willow. *Three-Toed Sloths (Up a Tree).* New York: Powerkids Press (2012).

Guidone, Julie. *Sloths (Animals that Live in the Rain Forest).* Pleasantville, NY: Weekly Reader Early Learning Library (2009).

Lunis, Natalie. *Three-Toed Sloths: Green Mammals (Disappearing Acts).* New York: Bearport (2010).

Learn more online

To learn more about three-toed sloths, visit
www.bearportpublishing.com/JungleBabies

About the author

Rachel Lynette has written more than 100 nonfiction books for children. She also creates resources for teachers. Rachel lives near Seattle, Washington. She enjoys biking, hiking, crocheting hats, and spending time with her family and friends.